PROPHET IDREES (A.S)

SEEMA SUHANA

Contents

Contents

Foreword

These books gives us knowledge about our beloved Prophets in story form . Books are available on all e-sites such as Amazon (India , USA , UK) , Flipkart (India) , Snapdeal (India) , Booktopia (UK,USA) , Barneandnoble(UK,USA) Shopee (India) ,wordery (USA) ,Wob (UK), Libro (USA) , Notionpress . contact me on instagram @Soulful_suhana to order in bulk and to get great discounts on it

(A.S)-Alaihi Salam

These books are available in English , Hindi , Roman Urdu

English :

Book 1 : Story of Prophet Adam (A.S)

Book 2: Prophet Sheesh (A.S)

Book 3: Prophet Idrees (A.S)

Book 4 :Strom of Prophet Nuh (A.S)

Book 5 : Journey from heaven to strom (Story of Prophet Adam (A.S) from heaven to Prophet Nuh (A.S) in floods and strom)

Roman Urdu

Book 1 : " Kahani Adam (A.S) Ki"

Book 2:"Hazrat Sheesh (A.S) "

Book 3: " Aknookh Yani Hazrat Idrees (A.S) "

Book 4 :"Toofan -e-Nuh "

(Story of Hazrat Nuh (A.S)"

Book 5 :"Arsh se Toofan Tak "

(Story of Hazrat Adam (A.S) in Jannah to Hazrat Nuh (A.S) In Floods And Strom)

Hindi

पुस्तक 1: पैगंबर आदम (अलैही सलाम) की कहानी

पुस्तक 2: पैगंबर शीश (अलैही सलाम)

पुस्तक 3: पैगंबर इदरीस (अलैही सलाम)

पुस्तक 4: पैगंबर नूह (अलैही सलाम) का तूफान

पुस्तक 5: जन्नत से तूफान तक

(पैगंबर आदम (अलैही सलाम) से पैगंबर नूह (अलैही सलाम) तक)

Acknowledgements

(A.S) Refers to Alaihi Salam

ALHAMDULLIAH FOR EVERYTHING

I also do Arabic calligraphy

Dm me to placed your customised order

Do follow me on

youtube channel: soulful suhana

instagram id : soulful_suhana

CHAPTER ONE

Prophet Idrees (A.S)

Prophet Idrees (A.S) was born in Babylon Prophet Idrees (A.S) real name is Anookh. Prophet Idrees (A.S) is included in the list of Prophets who's name is mentioned in the Qur'an. Prophet Idrees (A.S) came into world 500 years after the death of Prophet Adam (A.S)

Prophet Idrees (A.S) used to recite constantly the books of Allah that is why the name Idrees was titled to him and the name became so famous that many people do not even know real name. In Quran the name Idrees is mention .

Prophet Idrees (A.S), was declared a prophet in the time of Prophet Sheesh (A.S). Prophet Idrees (A.S) was the protector of the lessons of his ancestors. Prophet Idrees (A.S) acquired knowledge from his great-grandfather Prophet Sheesh (A.S). Through Prophet Idrees (A.S), Allah gave the treasure of knowledge to human beings.

At the time of Prophet Idrees (A.S) man fell into ignorance so much that they started worshiping fire instead of Allah. Prophet Idrees (A.S) came to the world and guided , instructed people taught literature, knowledge but the community of Prophet Idrees (A.S) did not listen . only few people believed in Prophet Idrees (A.S) .

Upon this, Prophet Idrees (A.S) was so mystify that he migrated from there with those who believed Prophet Idrees (A.S) from Babylon to Misr

CHAPTER TWO

From Prophet Adam (A.S) to Prophet Idrees (A.S)

Prophet Idrees (A.S) is from the generation of Anoosh, the son of Prophet Sheesh (A.S). Prophet Idrees's father's name was Yarid and his mother's name was Yarkana. Wife name of Prophet Idrees (A.S) is Aadna . There was also a son whose name is Muttashalak. 30 pages were revealed to Prophet Idrees (A.S). Prophet Idrees (A.S) was born 1000 years before Prophet Nuh (A.S)

Prophet Idrees (A.S), is the middle link of Prophet Nuh (A.S) and Prophet Adam (A.S)

Prophet Idrees (A.S) is from 6th generation after Prophet Adam (A.S)

Prophet Adam (A.S)

↓

Prophet Sheesh (A.S)

↓

ANOOSH

↓

Qinan

↓

Mahlaai

↓

Yarid

↓

Aknookh(Prophet Idrees (A.S))

CHAPTER THREE

Personality

Prophet Idrees (A.S) personality is described as follows full length and width, beautiful, heavenly soul , bushy beard, broad shoulder , strong bones , thin in size ,excellent humor , black sparkling eyes , peaceful lover, while walking looked down, accustomed to extreme thought and fear, Horridnesses when angry, accustomed to pointing index finger repeatedly while talking.

CHAPTER FOUR

Prophecy of Prophet Idrees (A.S)

When Prophet Sheesh (A.S) passed away, his followers were very few in number.

Adultery , Immodesty, atheistic ,drunkenness were commonly spread by children of kabeel

It was difficult to identify pure and true relationships. Worship of the Buddha (statue) and fire were taking place. Shaitan's ruled over the world

This was the time when Allah decided to send Prophet for people's guidance and avenge Prophet Idrees (A.S) from the descendants (children) of Prophet Sheesh (A.S). When Prophet Idrees (A.S) grew up, Allah Almighty blessed him with Prophethood.

Prophet Idrees (A.S) had all the qualities that a prophet should have. Prophet Idrees (A.S), was the protector of the religion of Prophet Adam (A.S) . Prophet Idrees (A.S) was very devout (worshipers), a very true human being.

Prophet Idrees (A.S) after being on Prophethood gave his guidance to people , invited them to religion of Islam and shared the knowledge of Prophet Sheesh (A.S) which he followed.

And after Prophet Sheesh (A.S) the descendants of Kabeel had gone astray and for their guidance Allah sent Prophet Idrees (A.S) as Prophet

CHAPTER FIVE

language

The language of Prophet Idrees (A.S) was Saryani. At the time of Prophet Idrees (A.S) there was 72 language spoken .Prophet Idrees (A.S) invited people to the religion of Islam in every language

CHAPTER SIX

Migration from Babylon

Prophet Idrees (A.S) forbade people to accompany Kabeel's people but very few people listened to Prophet Idrees (A.S).

The path of truth and words of goodness was unpleasant to the people, they became enemies of Prophet Idrees (A.S). Prophet Idrees (A.S) and his followers began to suffer in various ways until Prophet Idrees (A.S) became tired of their actions and decided to emigrate from Babylon.

Prophet Idrees (A.S) and his companion left Babylon. Some of the companions of Prophet Idrees (A.S) came and asked Prophet Idrees (A.S) " O Prophet of Allah Prophet Idrees (A.S) if we leave Babylon where we will find such a place?". Prophet Idrees (A.S) said, "If we hope in Allah, He will grant us everything that we wanted ." And left for Misr. Finally, Prophet Idrees (A.S) and his companion reached Misr . It was a very beautiful place at that time.

As soon as Prophet Idrees (A.S) reached there he thanked Allah and said Subhanallah .

Prophet Idrees (A.S) lived in Misr and fulfilled his prophecy duties .

CHAPTER SEVEN

Prophet Idrees (A.S) continued his work even after the migration

Prophet Idrees (A.S) and his preacher (companion) gave same teachings in Misr and invited them to believe in one God i.e., Allah . Prophet Idrees (A.S) taught them to get save from the hellfire and do good deeds.

Prophet Idrees (A.S) started teaching to the people. Prophet Idrees (A.S) started all efforts to prevent people from worshiping statues

Prophet Idrees (A.S) prevented people from accumulating into love of land, wealth, possessions and wealth . Prophet Idrees (A.S) instructed the people to stay away from alcohol. only few people accepted the teachings of Prophet Idrees (A.S) and became companions and others started going against them. The wave of enmity did not diminish, Prophet Idrees (A.S) would raise your level even higher and work harder to convey the teachings of Allah to people

Prophet Idrees (A.S) was great leader with kind nature. Prophet Idrees (A.S) made many new principles to persuade people to worship Allah, to believe in Allah and also instructed the people to avoid evil sins . Prophet Idrees (A.S) perform all his duties as a true Prophet would perform.

Prophet Idrees (A.S) followed Shari'ah of Prophet Sheesh (A.S) . As Prophet Idrees (A.S) was also the Rasool of Allah he would receive new principle , messages , rules from Allah . Prophet Idrees (A.S) would give all the knowledge , messages to people and convince them to in believe in Allah who is the only God .

Prophet Idrees (A.S) taught prayers . Prophet Idrees (A.S) also taught about fasting days in each month and instructed them to fight with the enemy.

Prophet Idrees (A.S) also emphasized on the cleanliness, ablution, purity

Dogs and other unclean animals meat are forbidden to eat. Prohibited alcohol and other intoxicants. Prophet Idrees (A.S) explained the ways of offering sacrifice . Emphasis was placed on the use of roses in flowers, wheat in grains and grapes in fruits

Prophet Idrees (A.S) also taught people about the development of the city and the knowledge of life. He also taught politics and its history.

Prophet Idrees (A.S) built 142 cities in his time and obtain Knowledge from it. Prophet Idrees (A.S) also had Expertness in astrology

Prophet Idrees (A.S) taught different tribes to live according to their needs. At that time, in terms of population, the land was divided into four parts and one ruler was appointed for each part of the land. It was the duty of this ruler to teach people manners and to live according to them.

Before Prophet Idrees (A.S) people used to make and wear clothes of the same age animal . Prophet Idrees (A.S) taught people about making of clothes and wearing it.

Prophet Idrees (A.S) traveled all over the world. Allah says in the Quran Surah -Al -Ambiya " all the prophets Prophet Ismail (A.S) , Prophet Zulfekaar (A.S) , and Prophet Idrees (A.S) , all these Prophets are Patient . And We have taken in our mercy, therefore all these prophets are on straight path "

CHAPTER EIGHT

Worship of Prophet Idrees (A.S)

Prophet Idrees (A.S) fasted very oftenly and recited 12000 tazbi every day. In the assembly of Prophet Idrees (A.S) angels would include themselves.

CHAPTER NINE

Mentioning of Jannah (heavens)

Prophet Idrees (A.S) used to say to his people that he had visited Jannah 30 times and he was aware of it.

CHAPTER TEN

Knowledge of Astrology

Prophet Idrees (A.S) was the first person to know astrology. If the Prophet had not been given this knowledge, then the guidance of man would have been difficult

CHAPTER ELEVEN

Angel of Death mentioning Prophet Idrees (A.S)

Once Angel of Death, ie Angel Izrael asked, "O Allah, who is your beloved servant in the earth whose deeds come from the Holy Spirit?"

Allah said, " Prophet Idrees (A.S) is my beloved servant"

CHAPTER TWELVE

The Holy Prophet Sallahu Alaihi Wasallam Mentioning Prophet Idrees (A.S)

It is narrated by some schlors that they asked the Holy Prophet Sallahu Alaihi Wasallam about the sand astrology . The Holy Prophet Sallahu Alaihi Wasallam said : " there was one Prophet in this world who wrote this and had knowledge about sand astrology " , so the person he mentioned was Prophet Idrees (A.S)

CHAPTER THIRTEEN

Usage of pen

In the hadith it is mention , after Prophet Adam (A.S) and Prophet Sheesh (A.S), Prophet Idrees (A.S) is the first prophet who wrote through Pen . Prophet Idrees (A.S) is the first person (man) who taught people to read and write, in that sense he is the teacher of the world.

CHAPTER FOURTEEN

Prophet Idrees (A.S) informed his People about the coming messenger

As long as Prophet Idrees (A.S) was present in this world, he told his people Allah has started a chain of sending Prophets in this world for peoples guidance and they will be abstinence from sins . They will share knowledge of eternal world ,mercy from it and they will be aware of the necessities of life in this world. They will be kept informed of the sufferings and cures of the people of this world. They will be available for healing . Their prayers will be answered by Allah , and they will know what is in the restoration of the world. "

CHAPTER FIFTEEN

The life of Prophet Idrees (A.S) in two parts

There were 2 things in the life of Prophet Idrees (A.S).

A.Tabliq (to reach out , let people be informed)

(Tabliq means to believe to reach out , let people be informed about one God and to worship Allah with all believes)

B. Jihad

15 A.Tabliq (to reach out , let people be informed)

Prophet Idrees (A.S) had mastery in tabliq . Prophet Idrees (A.S) first effort was to through tabliq , he could get kabeel's children on the right path and the world would became pure and devoted to the worship of One God i.e., Allah , but Shaitan took them in his grip.

When Prophet Idrees (A.S) used to talk about Allah, he advise to worship Allah, stay away from sins then these words were Unbearable by them . They would get red in anger and make Prophet Idrees (A.S) suffer pain ,laugh at him , beat with stones .

after living with the shaitan for a long time, these people have become entangled themselves with disbelief and evil sins .

The world was divided into two parts , one following Shaitan and the other believing in Allah and His Prophet.

Prophet Idrees (A.S) used to be very sad and upset about this situation

15 b. Jihad

When Prophet Idrees (A.S) saw that the disbelievers were oppressing the believers. Prophet Idrees (A.S) tried his best to bring the people to the right path through tabliq, but their unpleasantness. distastefulness. foulness. horribleness. was spreading day by day and in spite of socialization, people were not choosing the right path .By Allah's command Prophet Idrees (A.S) to wage jihad against against those people who were destroying peace

Prophet Idrees (A.S) fought against the people of kabeel with a group of young people who believed in Allah and His Messenger . In this jihad Allah granted Prophet Idrees (A.S) with success and many people repented and believed in Allah and in his messenger.

For jihad Prophet Idrees (A.S) first prepared an army , then divided it into two parts . One part with soldiers on foot they are called as Foot soldiers , the other part soldiers on horses they are called as cavalry, after tremendous training Prophet Idrees (A.S) did opening of jihad the first move .

Fight was on for the justice and peace and in the end Prophet Idrees (A.S) forced them to kneel down and looted wealth and made them slaves

Prophet Idrees (A.S) was the first person who fought in the way of Allah , gained -plunder ,prize , boon and made his enemies slaves but -plunder , prize , boon and slaves were not permissible for him.

The Holy Prophet Sallallahu Alaihi Wasalllam is the first Messenger for whom plunder , prize , boon was made lawful, but it is certain that the first jihad was carried out by Prophet Idrees (A.S).

CHAPTER SIXTEEN

Special work of Prophet Idrees (A.S)

Prophet Idrees (A.S) spent his whole life teaching people, because that is the purpose of the life of a true prophet.

- *Prophet Idrees (A.S) not only taught the people about the measurements but also taught them tips and tricks of correct measurements.*

- *It was Prophet Idrees (A.S) who informed the people about the stars in peoples life*

- *Usuage of pen*

- *Prophet Idrees (A.S) was the best rider, the people before Prophet Idrees (A.S) did not know how to ride, and could not even do*

- *Prophet Idrees (A.S) is the first person in all of humanity who taught people to make weapons for hunting.*

- *It was Prophet Idrees (A.S) who started the process of teaching religion to the people did tabliq and invited people to the religion of Islam*

- *Jihad*

- *Prophet Idrees (A.S) always advised his people not to go to near Goofiness, otherwise knowledge will be lacking.*

- *Prophet Idrees (A.S) used to say that it is necessary to remember Allah and do good deeds*

- *Prophet Idrees used to say do not swear falsely and do not persuade people to swear.*

-

Prophet Idrees (A.S) used to say one should respect elders , do good deeds and keep on praising Allah and remember Him at all times.

-

Don't be jealous when you see wealth and prosperity of others

CHAPTER SEVENTEEN

characteristical (specialities)

Here are the 11 characteristical pleasures that Allah is given to Prophet Idrees (A.S)

1. Prophet Idrees (A.S) is included in the list of Prophets mentioned in the Qur'an.

2. Prophet Idrees (A.S) was the Prophet After Prophet Sheesh (A.S)

3. There were 30 parts , pages (saheefe) sent to Prophet Idrees (A.S)

4. Prophet Idrees (A.S) introduced astrology to the world

5. Prophet Idrees (A.S) was the first to introduced usage of pen and to write in the world

6. Prophet Idrees (A.S) also taught to stitch clothes .

7. Prophet Idrees (A.S) made weapons for war

8. Prophet Idrees (A.S) issued the Sunnah of Jihad

9. Prophet Idrees (A.S) made the cruel humans as slaves after jihad

10. Prophet Idrees (A.S) also taught riding

11. Prophet Idrees (A.S) did tabliq called upon people to believe in one and true God i.e., Allah

CHAPTER EIGHTEEN

The teachings of Prophet Idrees (A.S)

Here are some lessons from Prophet Idrees (A.S) in which we could get instructions till the day of Judgement.

- *The better of those who keep an eye on their qualities and use them for their own pleasure.*

- *There is no one better who shares blessings of Allah with other servants*

- *Don't get angry or jealous of anything that other posses. This is just a temporary thing*

-

The one who wants too much, he will not be able to get much benefit from it

•

There is no best blessing than wisdom

Allah has not mentioned all these things but Allah has mentioned about Prophet Idrees (A.S) in his book Qur'an. In Sureh Maryam verse no 56,57 " And mention in the Book ?O Prophet, the story of? Idrees . He was surely a man of truth and a prophet. " , "And We elevated him to an honourable status."

There is mention in Bukhari about his high position

The Holy Prophet Sallahu Alaihi Wasallam said " I met Prophet Idrees (A.S) on 4th level jannah in the night of the Mehraj . , he is at honourabl status at 4th level of jannah"

CHAPTER NINETEEN

Journey towards the sky

Prophet Idrees (A.S) lives 365 years in this world and then

Prophet Idrees (A.S) was taken up to the heavens by Allah

There are three stories of Prophet Idrees (A.S) being taken to heaven , allah knows which one is true among them

A. Prophet Idrees (A.S) in 4th level of jannah and the time of blink of an eye

Prophet Idrees (A.S) was the ultimate worshiper. once Allah revealed ,conveyed message through Angel Jibreel " o Idrees I will grant you good deeds which are equal to all good deeds that world does in a day "

When Prophet Idrees (A.S) received this good news from Allah, he was overjoyed. After that, his heart wanted him to worship more for the sake of Allah so that his deeds would increase further. In the hope to increase his good deeds he asked his angel friend who used to visit Prophet Idrees (A.S) frequently

Prophet Idrees (A.S) said to his friend Angel Allah has sent me this message through Angel Jibreel that " Allah will grant me good deeds which are equal to all good deeds that world does in a day ", so you should make a meeting of mine with Angel of death Angel Izrael because I want to ask him about my life , How many days are left in my life so that good deeds increases with each passing day .

Hearing this, his friend Angel picked Prophet Idrees (A.S) up on his lap, carried him on his arm (shoulder) and ascended to the sky.

At the time when Prophet Idrees (A.S) was ascended to heaven, he was 365 years old. When Prophet Idrees (A.S) friend Angel reached 4th level of jannah , he saw Angel of death Angel Izrael coming downstairs of jannah

friend Angel of Prophet Idrees (A.S), asked Angel of Death how much more life of Prophet Idrees (A.S) was left.?

Angel Israel said to him, "Why are you asking me?" ?

Friend Angel said It is Prophet Idrees (A.S) who asked me to take ask you about his life

Hearing this,Angel Izreel asked friend angel of Prophet Idrees (A.S) to tell him where Prophet Idrees (A.S) himself was present at that time.

Angel friend replied, "At this moment he is riding on my back."

Wow, this is very strange Angel Izrael said

The angel friend of Prophet Idrees (A.S) said: What is strange in this?

Angel Izrael told him that " Allah had just ordered him to take soul of Prophet Idrees (A.S) on 4th level of jannah " Upon hearing this command, I was amazed that Prophet Idrees (A.S) is on earth. Allah has ordered me to take soul of Prophet Idrees (A.S) on 4th level of Jannah .

After hearing the command of Allah without asking any question I started walking towards of the heavens. Now I got why Allah commanded me to take soul of Prophet Idrees (A.S) on 4th level of jannah as Prophet Idrees (A.S) is present already here

Angel friend of Prophet Idrees (A.S) asked " how much time Prophet Idrees had left.?"

Angel Izrael said only " only blink of eye time is left "

Angel of Death (Angel Izrael) came near Prophet Idrees (A.S) and asked for his permission and took his soul.

Prophets had the privilege that the Angel cannot take their soul without their permission

The Holy Prophet Sallalahu Alaihi Wasallam was given the option to stay in this world as long as he wanted, or to choose Allah

The Holy Prophet Sallalahu Alaihi Wasallam choosed death , choosed Allah.

Thus Prophet Idrees (A.S) soul was taken on 4th level of jannah .

Like Prophet Essa (A.S) , Prophet Idrees (A.S) was taken up to heaven. The difference is that the soul of Prophet Essa (A.S) was not taken

Then Angel friend of Prophet Idrees (A.S) saw Prophet Idrees (A.S) who was on his back , he saw Prophet Idrees (A.S) was dead

And then Angel Izrael returned to the first level of jannah

B. Prophet Idrees (A.S) in 4th level of jannah , visiting to heaven and hell

Prophet Idrees (A.S) used to live in the worship of Allah , he was ultimate worshiper and he was also looked upon with love and respect by angels. Angels frequently visited Prophet Idrees (A.S) and used to spend time with him.

Once Angel Izrael also came with the permission of Allah and stayed with Prophet Idrees (A.S) for a long time in human form.

When Prophet Idrees (A.S) found out that he was not a human being but Angel Izrael and was in the service of capturing the soul of living beings

Prophet Idrees (A.S) said to Angel of death (Angel Izrael), "I want to taste death , you take my soul from body after capturing the soul again return back to me "

Angel Izrael did as per the instructions of Prophet Idrees (A.S) . Angel Izrael took soul and returned the soul to Prophet Idrees (A.S) .

Then Prophet Idrees (A.S) requested Angel Izrael | "take me through hell so that I fear Allah more And I worship Allah as much as possible "

Angel Izrael also obeyed this order too and took Prophet Idrees (A.S) through hell . Seeing hell, Prophet Idrees (A.S) said, "Open this door and I want to pass through this door too" Angel Izrael obeyed this instruction too.

Prophet Idrees (A.S) said to Angel Izrael Show me Paradise. Angel Izrael took Prophet Idrees (A.S) to Paradise.

After waiting for a while, Angel Izrael said to Prophet Idrees (A.S) " let's go back to your place "

Prophet Idrees (A.S) said to Angel Izrael " I will not leave this place now. Allah has said " every soul shall taste death " and I have tasted death once . Allah also said "every person has to go through hell" and I have passed through hell

Now I have reached Paradise and Allah has said "to those who reach Paradise that those who enter Paradise will not be expelled from Paradise."

Now why are you asking me to leave jannah ? Allah sent message to Angel Izrael " Whatever Idrees did, he did it with my knowledge and will, and with my permission he entered Paradise, so he will remain in Paradise. "

C. Meeting traveller and then visiting hell, heaven

Prophet Idrees (A.S) used to live in the worship of Allah , he was ultimate worshiper and he was also looked upon with love and respect by angels. Angels frequently visited Prophet Idrees (A.S) and used to spend time with him.

One day, by the command of Allah, Angel of death , Angel Izrael became an old traveler and knocked on the door of Prophet Idrees (A.S). Prophet Idrees (A.S) opened the door and thus Angel of death , Angel Izrael became the guest of Prophet Idrees (A.S)

As Prophet Idrees (A.S) was fasting and it was time for Iftar, all the food used to come to Prophet Idrees (A.S) from heaven .

Prophet Idrees (A.S) would eat as much as he wanted from that food and the rest would go back to heaven

On that day too food came from heaven, Prophet Idrees (A.S) placed that food in front of the old traveller, but that traveller was constantly engaged in worship and did not even see this food.

Prophet Idrees (A.S) was Surprised and the night passed, when morning came Prophet Idrees (A.S) said to old traveller , "Come, guest, we are going out. I will show you the beautiful world that Allah has created."

While walking, they came to the across of a yarn of wheat, and there the old traveler said to Prophet Idrees (A.S) " Why don't we eat some of the wheat from here? "

Prophet Idrees (A.S) said " I am surprised that I kept food in front of you at night and you did not touch it and now you are talking about to eat haraam food."

After walking further, they came across a garden, where the traveler saw the grapes tree and wished to eat it.

Prophet Idrees (A.S) said " it is haraam to take fruit and eat without permission "

Again after walking for a while Angel Izrael who disguised as an old traveler saw a goat , he intended to eat it.

Prophet Idrees (A.S) said " it is haraam to eat a unknown goat that does not belong to you "

Both of them continued talking for three days

When Prophet Idrees (A.S) found out who this person was as Angel Izrael does not seemed to be one of the children of Prophet Adam . Prophet Idrees (A.S) said, " for Allah's sake tell me who you are ?

On listening Prophet Idrees (A.S) words Angel Izrael said " I am Angel Izrael ." Then Prophet Idrees (A.S) said, " you are the one who take the souls of all creatures." Angel Izrael said, "Yes."

Prophet Idrees (A.S) said " are you here to take my soul ? "

Angel Izrael said, "No, I have come to spend time with you."

Prophet Idrees (A.S) said " you been with me for three days during this period have you taken soul of any creature "

Angel Izrael (A.S) said " kaula -kulla-ha-bayna-ya -daiyaaa-ha ka-anna -maa -bi-yaa-di-ka -khubzan" which means " food under both hands , that is by the command of Allah, whose time has arrived I will take their life ."

Angel Izrael said, " O Prophet Idrees (A.S), I want to build a cordial relationship with you "

Prophet Idrees (A.S) said " I will have a cordial relationship with you only when you give me the taste of death once so that the fear of Allah increases and I may worship my creator more."

Angel of death said " I cannot take anyone's life without any reason " . Then Prophet Idrees (A.S) prayed to Allah and Allah commanded Angel Izrael to do things as per Prophet Idrees (A.S) wish

Prophet Idrees (A.S) soul was taken and he was dead and then Angel Izrael prayed to Allah .

Allah accepted Angel Izrael prayer and Prophet Idrees (A.S) got up and took Angel Izrael in his arms.

Prophet Idrees (A.S) and Angel Izrael established their Relationships

Then Angel Izrael asked Prophet Idrees (A.S) , "O brother, what is it like when soul is been seprated ?

Prophet Idrees (A.S) said " like the skin of a living animal being pulled from head to toe "

Angel Izrael said " I swear of Allah like I have done this to you I have not done this to anyone "

Prophet Idrees (A.S) said, "O my brother, I am fond of seeing Hell, so take me to its gates so that I may have more fear of Allah by seeing it, and that will increase my devotion to worship Allah."

By the permission of Allah Angel Izrael showed 7 levels (doors) of Hell to Prophet Idrees (A.S)

Then Prophet Idrees (A.S) said " Open this door and I want to pass through this door." Angel Izrael did the same.

Death of Angel (Angel Izrael) took Prophet Idrees (A.S) to jannah . After waiting for a while, Angel Izrael said " o

Prophet Idrees (A.S) " let's go back to your place we have to leave this place now " .

Prophet Idrees (A.S) said " I will not leave this place now Allah has said Kullu nafasaatin maut which means every soul shall taste death and I have tasted death and Allah also said Every person has to go through hell" and I have passed

From hell too. Now I have reached jannah and Allah has said to those who reach jannah that those who enter jannah will not be expelled from jannah . "

Now why are you asking me to come out of Paradise (jannah) ? Allah sent message through wahi to Angel Izrael

Whatever " Prophet Idrees (A.S) did, he did it with my knowledge and will, and with my permission he entered Paradise, so he will remain in Paradise. "

CHAPTER TWENTY

Shaitan's ways to associate people with shrik i.e., not believeing in Allah

Shaitan brought people towards shrik in three different ways at three different times A.

A.Worshiping fire by Kabeel

B. Worshiping budh statue in the times of Prophet Adam (A.S)

C. During the time of Prophet Idrees (A.S)

20 A . worshiping fire by Kabeel

After the incident of qurbani , Shaitan came to kabeel in human form and said, "The fire has eaten habeel's sacrifice, because he worships fire, so you worship too." Kabeel is the first person to worship fire so he is the first person to disobey Allah

Kabeel first started worshipping fire leaving all his father's religious authority behind.

20 B. Worshiping budh statue in the times of Prophet Adam (A.S)

There were some good people between Prophet Adam (A.S) and Prophet Sheesh (A.S) and others used to praise them for their good deeds and follow them.

Budha was a noble person, and he was a very beloved person of his people. When he died, his people his follower would sit surrounded by his grave and wipe tears

When shaitan saw them, he came as a man in human form and said, "I saw you crying, so what do you think ? , I can and want to make a picture of Budh for you?"

you keep this picture of him in your assembly and remember him when you see it in your assembly.

They agreed with the Shaitan So he made a picture of this noble man.

followers said, "If we keep his picture , we will have more passion in our prayers ."

And they used to keep the picture of Budh in their assembly and offer their prayers

And when they died and the second generation came, the shaitan explained them that their ancestors were worshipping picture.

When shaitaan saw this scene, of people sitting in the assembly worshipping the picture, he said to them , " should I keep a Budh's statue in every house of yours."

They agreed to shaitan's word and every one of them kept budh's statue in one's house thus budh's was mentioned in every house.

Then their children were said same thing by shaitan and practiced same then next generations came , they forgot that budh was a Noble man.

They brought him to worship as God, and then they began to worship this god, denying Allah . Thus the first one to be prayed was the Budh a noble man who later was called God Budh .

20 .C During the time of Prophet Idrees (A.S)

When Prophet Idrees (A.S) ascended to the heavens with his Angel friend and did not return, his sons and relatives became very upset.

In this case Shaitan came to them in his human form and said " Your father is dead and he will never come back to this world . I Will do one thing that will lighten your grief , I will make a picture of Prophet Idrees (A.S) and give it to you so that you can see it and lighten your grief. "

Prophet Idrees (A.S) sons said " that will very good thing, so Shaitan made a picture of Prophet Idrees (A.S) and gave it to them. They were very happy to see this picture.

Shaitan (Iblees) made picture so accurate the only diiference was Prophet Idrees (A.S) Picture could not speak

Then, if another good man from the community of Prophet Idrees (A.S) had died, Shaitan would have done the same to them i.e., made a picture of him and handed it over to their children.

CHAPTER TWENTY-ONE

People forgotten Allah

People lived on monotheism for 1000 years after the death of Prophet Adam (A.S) . People were involved in sinful acts but they were not disbeliever of Allah.

When the idols of their forefathers became common everywhere, they were worshiped at all times and in all places. By continous worshiping statues people forgot Allah who is the one and only God

It has been a long time since Prophet Idrees (A.S) died and no other prophet came in his place, so worshiping statue and evil acts spread everywhere.

9 798887 334981

Printed by Libri Plureos GmbH in Hamburg, Germany